DESIGN OF MY WORLD

DESIGN OF MY WORLD

H. B. DEHQANI-TAFTI

THE SEABURY PRESS • NEW YORK

1982
The Seabury Press
815 Second Avenue
New York, N.Y. 10017

Copyright © 1959 by H. B. Dehqani-Tafti
Introduction copyright © 1982 by H. B. Dehqani-Tafti
All rights reserved. No part of this book may be reproduced, stored in a retrieval system, or transmitted, in any form or by any means, electronic, mechanical, photocopying, recording or otherwise, without the written permission of The Seabury Press.

Printed in the United States of America

Library of Congress Cataloging in Publication Data

Dehqani-Tafti, H. B. (Hassan B.)
Design of my world.
1. Dehqani-Tafti, H. B. (Hassan B.)
2. Anglican Communion—Bishops—Biography.
3. Bishops—Iran—Biography.   I. Title.
BX5680.6.Z8D44   1981   283'.3 [B]   81-5703
ISBN 0-8164-2346-6   AACR2

CONTENTS

Chapter   *Page*

    FOREWORD   7

1 FROM YEZD TO ISFAHAN: HOME AND HERITAGE   9

2 IN ISFAHAN TO CHRIST: STRUGGLE AND FAITH   23

3 WITH CHRIST THROUGH DESPAIR: ADVERSITY AND TRUST   37

4 TO ISFAHAN IN MINISTRY: THE CALL TO INTERPRET   57

The Biblical quotations in this book are taken from the Revised Standard Version of the Bible.

FOREWORD

People can have one of the two following viewpoints on their lives:

One is that of a cynic exemplified by a line from Nezami, a Persian poet, who sang some seven hundred years ago,

> Where do we go from here?
> Why did we come? Why do we go?
> We do not know!

The other is from Isaiah, one of the Prophets of Israel who lived about seven hundred years before Christ. He wrote regarding his mission in life,

> From birth the Lord called me,
> He named me from my mother's womb....
> He said to me, you are my servant....
> I will make you a light to the nations....
> Isaiah 49:1, 3,6

While I have often pondered on Nezami's viewpoint, and have allowed my mind to wander, trying to find an answer to the poet's riddle, I have counted myself fortunate enough to have had the belief, like Isaiah, that my coming into this world has been for a purpose. Over twenty years ago I tried to relate the pattern of this purpose in *Design of My World*. The design did not stop when the book was published, but went on quietly, smoothly and unobtrusively until two years ago when, like a silent volcano which suddenly erupts, the whole pattern of my life was caught up in the fires of the Iranian Revolution.

I am glad for the opportunity to see a new edition of *Design of My World* at this time.

H. B. Dehqani-Tafti
Bishop in Iran
Cambridge, England
February 1981

CHAPTER ONE

FROM YEZD TO ISFAHAN: HOME AND HERITAGE

Travellers who come to Persia will almost certainly visit Teheran the capital, and Isfahan, and Shiraz, so famous for their history, their beauty and the place they hold as the centres of Persian craftsmanship and modern progress. But my boyhood and earliest affections belong to Taft, a village south-west of Yezd in central Iran.

Yezd, which bears the ancient Persian name for God—Izzed—is a quiet city where the people are industrious and thrifty, working long hours at their looms weaving cotton and silk materials, or else cultivating the hard dry earth which upon being watered is amazingly fertile.

Taft lies beyond the Yezd desert, in the foothills of a great range of mountains, with two high and barren peaks bearing the names of Lion Mountain and the Snow House. The village is built on the banks of a great dry stony riverbed, which fills with flood waters when the winter snows melt upon the high slopes in the spring. Then Taft breaks into beauty; the orchards are pink with peach blossom and the pomegranate trees glisten in the sunshine, their brilliant scarlet flowers aflame in the fresh foliage. The houses are simple, of sun-dried mud-brick behind high mud walls; the narrow streets are dusty, and underneath them run the deep streams of water artificially dug for the purpose.

Our home had but two rooms and a kitchen, and I can well remember my mother Sekineh working there. One of the rooms was her dispensary; people of all kinds came to her and called upon her for help, for she had some knowledge of modern nursing, and at that time Taft had no hospital. Where had my mother obtained her knowledge of nursing?

Before the first world war the first hospital had been built in Yezd by Christian missionaries, and the fame of its doctors and nurses had spread far and wide. My grandmother, who was able to read and recite the Holy Quran and for that reason was known as "Mulla Zahra", in her old age had something the matter with her eyes. She needed treatment, so one day she and her two daughters Sekineh and Rubabeh set out upon a venture which was to be the foundation of the pattern of life for me.

When Mulla Zahra and her two daughters arrived in Yezd the Christian hospital received them all, the mother as a patient and the daughters as her nurses, who later on were to be trained as nurses for the hospital.

Years passed by. Thousands were being healed; the gospel of love was being preached every day through the loving actions of the doctors and sisters and through the words of the evangelists and ministers of the Church. The task of building up the Church of Jesus Christ in the Yezd of that day was even more formidable than it is to-day. It needs two very special gifts of the Holy Spirit, patience and humility; and that means being ready to work for a lifetime without necessarily seeing any results. Fortunately these few missionaries in that remote part of the world seem to have been endowed with those gifts—they were specialists of the impossible. Through their selfless service and faithful teaching, here and there individuals would come, sometimes out of curiosity, sometimes for mixed motives, and sometimes sincerely.

The mystic-loving people of Persia would naturally be inclined to love what is essentially a mystic religion, i.e. Christianity. A people who through their long history have suffered much cannot be indifferent to the Cross of Jesus once they *see* it. But there's the rub! If they see it! The sun was hidden behind the thick clouds of suspicion. Pride, arrogance, and domination from the West—in the East hatred, revenge and the wrong kind of lowliness, which springs from poverty and not from true humility. But the missionaries went on in spite of all this; and the loveliness of the mystic Christ and the meaning of His Cross would every now and then shine through the thick clouds and gently and miraculously open up a humble and sensitive heart.

One of these hearts must have been Sekineh's. No amount of suspicion, hatred and misunderstanding could have prevented her simple and affectionate soul from seeing through the clouds the love of God revealed in Jesus. She was baptized and confirmed, and later on was taught to read and write. Quietly she must have suffered a great deal at the hands of her relatives; but in that small community of Christians in Yezd she felt safe, and serving her Lord and her fellow-countrymen by nursing in the hospital she was happy. But this state of affairs did not last long.

In 1914, war broke out between Germany and Britain. Turkey was Germany's ally and Persia's neighbour. There was bound to be trouble in Persia. The Turks and the Germans created unrest, and the missionaries in the south of Persia who were British had to evacuate the country. War was being waged in Europe, and the Christian hospital in Yezd had to be closed down!

Within a few weeks the two hospitals in Yezd were closed, the missionaries had left, and the still infant local church disorganized. Mulla Zahra once again took her two daughters and travelled back to Taft. Deep changes must have occurred within them as the result of their contact with the missionaries and others in the hospital. Both Sekineh and her sister Rubabeh with their scanty knowledge of medicine started to practise nursing in their own village and the villages around. But usually girls cannot remain unmarried in villages. For Rubabeh it cannot have been a very grave problem, but for Sekineh it was. The only Christian girl in the Taft of that day! Whom was she going to marry? Sekineh, who to a large extent had been cut off from her own people and her own cultural and social environment in the deepest thing of life, namely religion, was happy and contented while she was part of a small living community—the Christian Church. But once she was back in her old surroundings, she was bound to a great extent to take on again the old colour. How much of her Christianity distinctly remained and how much of it was lost no one can exactly say. She was eventually married to a relative of hers in Taft. Muhammad was the name of her husband, an illiterate but intelligent young man, whose deep interest in his religion had made him loved and respected among those who knew him. Soon they had a son whom they called Yahya (John), and another one who was named Hassan. Another boy and then a girl were added to the family.

At last in 1918 the war ended. The missionaries came back to Yezd, the hospital was re-opened, and church services were started. Itineration was much more possible in those days, and the missionaries did not lose any opportunity. Miss W. A. Kingdon, the evangelist of the mission of that time, was very keen on this kind of work, going on her donkey from village to village in and around Yezd. A few incidents from her diary will make this plain;

"December 6th to 10th, 1921. Khalilabad. 4 Farsakhs [approximately 12 miles]. S. and A. went with me. 6th went to B's house, but only 3 or 4 came. Spoke on the blind man, Bartimaeus. 7th had a little talk outside B's house to little group, sang and spoke on the Birth. Went to Hosaini—had a little meeting in the village—had a talk with an old man who had been to Bombay. He bought a tract. Sang and talked of Lost Sheep. Asked where they were going after death they said 'namidanim' (we don't know). Promised to go again on Friday..."

"May 25th. Taft. Baghi Gulistan. Sekineh and Nazanin came about 3.30, had tea with me. Then I went with them to see their houses and they came back here for a meeting. Not very many, about 20—mostly Parsees."

"May 29th. Sekineh and Nazanin came for reading. Then I went to Sekineh's house where we had a nice little meeting, about 25 or so. They listened well."

So the words of the Gospel were echoed in our home when I was about one year old, for I was born in May 1920, and the Sekineh mentioned in Miss Kingdon's diary was my mother.

I have many memories of my childhood. I can well remember that, when I was about four years old, crowds of sick people used to come to our house where my mother's dispensary was. She has remained in my mind as the central figure to whom everybody referred his or her problem. Her figure is vivid in my memory, always on the move, trying to do what she could, quietly and kindly.

In the evenings my father used to light the oil lamp with much care and ceremony; we used to watch him intently and say "Salaam" when it was lit. We had been taught to greet the light in the same way as we greeted people. This may have been from recollection of a Parsee custom. Then we would squat around that lamp and listen to the stories that the grown-ups would tell. The stories were mainly of a religious nature, and mostly those common to both Christians and Muslims with some variation. I can well remember Yahya, my elder brother, trying to do his homework and at the same time telling us the story of the birth of John the Baptist, this time almost exactly as it is recorded in St. Luke's Gospel.

My happiness as a child came to an end when I was about five years old. It was night. We were all asleep on the roof of our house under the clear and starry sky; all except mother, who was ill in bed downstairs on the open space in front of the rooms. Suddenly a shriek followed by loud wailing noises woke us up. Father got up, looking very miserable and helpless, and went downstairs. I asked him whether I could go down with him, but he said that I had better go to sleep again, which I did. The next morning I asked for my mother, but she had gone for ever and I was to see her no more on this earth. Tuberculosis seems to have been the cause of her death.

The loss of his mother is one of the worst things that can happen to any child; but it is an even worse tragedy if it happens in a poor and primitive society, where a great deal of the well-being of the home and almost the entire happiness of early childhood depends on her. The death of my mother when I was still very young was a tragedy of this type; and yet God brought good out of that evil, as we shall see later on in these pages.

Our home life as we knew it with our mother as the centre was soon disorganized. Her knowledge of medicine and nursing, scanty as it was, had been among other things a source of income, making the family rather more comfortably off. Now that had stopped and my father had to work much harder; but no matter how hard he worked, we were always on the fringe of poverty. Yahya soon had to stop going to school, and had to work in order that he might at least earn his own living; and our only sister died when she was still a baby. I was not yet old enough to earn my living, nor was I young enough to die like my sister from lack of care and attention. I was just growing haphazardly, like one of the many thousands of thorn bushes growing in the deserts around Taft.

Towns and villages in Iran from the ancient days have been divided into districts very much like "parishes" in England. Each so-called parish has its mosque, and the mosque has its "incumbent". Also there is a sort of square in each "parish", where most of the open-air religious meetings and processions take place. Almost the entire social life of the "parish" is religious, and it is mostly concentrated in the mosque and the square.

Our small but very active "parish", with its mosque and its square, has vivid memories for me. My father was illiterate, but because of his good voice and a keen memory and his own interest in religion, he often used to take part in the religious activities of our "parish"; and he used to take me with him to them.

One of these in which I took part was the processions of the 10th of Muharram, the commemoration of the death of Imam Hussain the son of Ali. The more orthodox religious leaders have never been in favour of such processions, because they tend to encourage "religion through pictures", "acting" and "drama", and these things are contrary to the puritanical spirit in Islam. But Persian artistic taste and love of poetry and drama could not be eternally imprisoned. They could not have secular drama, but they took the most dramatic subject in their religious history and made a "Passion Play" out of it.

The original sad story runs as follows: Ali was the Prophet's son-in-law, and in the eyes of the Shi'ites his true successor. Ali had two sons, Hassan and Hussain. Hussain's wife was the daughter of Yezdigird, the last Persian king, who had been defeated by the Arabs. Persians have had a special love for the Household of Ali. Imam Hassan abdicated after he became Caliph, shortly after his father was attacked by one of the members of the opposing party and as a result died from his wounds. Then it was Imam Hussain's turn, and he would not abdicate although the enemy was much stronger. He stood up for what he believed to be his rights, and as the opposition was persistent, fighting was inevitable. By noon the fighting was over; Hussain was brutally killed and his body trampled under foot by his enemies. This happened in the month of Muharram on the tenth day. The Shi'ites believe that Imam Hussain died for nothing but the truth, and that therefore his death has sacrificial value; they ascribe to it some of the meanings that Christians ascribe to the Cross of Jesus Christ. To commemorate this tragic event and to mourn for it every year they have special ceremonies, one of these being the above-mentioned "Passion Play" in which all the events of the original day are re-enacted.

In the Taft of my childhood, everybody took part in these processions either by acting as one of the characters, or by watching it with heart and soul. Soon after my mother died one of these processions took place, and though I was so young I remember taking part in it. I was dressed up as Sekineh, one of the young daughters of Imam Hussain, and was put on a camel with another child who was supposed to be the other daughter. At the climax of this procession my part was to weep and ask for water, and the man was supposed not to give us any water and to pretend to be beating us up. I remember doing my part very well and quite naturally, because I was really thirsty and also frightened. The man who was supposed to be beating us took pity on me; he lifted me down and put me out of the circle which served as a stage, whereupon I took refuge under a big pulpit until the whole show was over and my father took me home.

When there were no religious activities either to watch or to take part in, I used to play in the square of our "parish" with other children. On most days I used to go to my uncle's shop with my grandfather to blow the bellows when they made spades, nails or other tools, for they were blacksmiths. I used to help with the farming in my cousin's gardens, pruning, gathering up the weeds, and looking after the donkeys so that the grown-ups might be able to pick the pomegranates from the trees. Sometimes I went with other children, taking the sheep out to give them water at the big pool in our neighbourhood. Later on this memory became somehow connected with the 23rd Psalm:

> "The LORD is my shepherd, I shall not want; he makes me lie down in green pastures. He leads me beside still waters; he restores my soul . . ."

Often some spiritual truth in the Bible applies exactly to someone's particular situation, and in my case the following verse from Amos 7 : 14 applied literally:

> "Then Amos answered Amaziah, 'I am no prophet, nor a prophet's son; but I am a herdsman, and a dresser of sycamore trees, and the LORD took me from following the flock, and the LORD said to me, 'Go, prophesy to my people Israel.'"

The Lord literally *took* me from tending the trees and following the flock and said to me "*Go* prophesy to my people." But this did not happen overnight. The process of the *taking* and the *saying* from the Lord's side and finally the *going* from my side have been rather a long and at times somewhat painful process.

Before my mother died, a few of her friends accompanied by the doctor in charge of the women's hospital in Yezd went to Taft to visit her. It was during that visit that she asked her Christian friends to see to it that among her children I at least should be brought up as a Christian. The only way to fulfil this wish of hers was for me to be sent to a Christian school. Who would take on such a responsibility, and would my father allow it? Those who are familiar with Muslim countries know how impossible it is for a Muslim father to let his child be taken away from him by non-Muslims for education. But those who are also familiar with the English character know that once an English person decides to do something he or she goes on and on until the thing is done. This characteristic, baptized in Christ, is a very great blessing, and Miss Kingdon seemed to have been very highly endowed with that quality. Her faith in God, her love for my mother and her desire to fulfil that last wish made her go on and on pressing my father to let me go to Yezd for education.

Both sides had quite a long time at their disposal,

for I was as yet too young to go to school. In the end, when I was six and a half years old, my father took refuge in consulting the Holy Quran, a custom often followed in Muslim villages by those who are in doubt about some decision. Much to the joy of Miss Kingdon and other friends of my mother, the result of the consultation came out as "good". Had the Holy Book been opened a page or two this way or that way, the result might have been "bad", and the end of all hopes for a Christian education for me. But when God, who rules all history, has a design for someone, who are we to say that He does not rule the opening of the pages of the Quran by a Mulla?

Miss Kingdon had to go step by step. There was no Christian boys' school in Yezd, but there was a Christian girls' school. Arrangements were made that I should go to that school. A Persian Christian couple from Isfahan, who had just married and set up house and were working in the mission hospital in Yezd, agreed to take me into their home.

Everything was arranged; and my father agreed to take me himself to Yezd. There were the two of us, father and son, crossing the fifteen miles of desert from Taft to Yezd; in the darkness of night to avoid the heat, under that fascinating starry sky. I either walked with my father or was carried on his shoulders.

My memories of the school in Yezd are very happy ones. We were taught the Persian alphabet by the Principal herself. I remember our Bible classes, and how tears came to my eyes as I listened to the story of Joseph and his brothers. We were encouraged to learn some of the Psalms by heart, a thing which I have never regretted and I wish that I had learned more. As it was a girls' school, in the afternoons we mostly did sewing, and I remember how proud I was of the cloth bag I had made and the handkerchief I had embroidered. But above all things I loved pencils and white paper. Apparently at times I used to spend the money given me for lunch to buy these two items.

Of church activities I remember very little, except that people were busy building a new grand church, which unfortunately a flood carried away some sixteen years later. A small Bible class for boys, and meetings for hymn singing and magic lantern shows, seem to be vaguely connected in my mind with those days in Yezd.

The home I was staying in was not an ideal place for a little boy whose mother had recently died. Husband and wife were recently married, and much more preoccupied with their new home and the arrival of their first baby than with attending to a boy from outside. However, the couple had their Persian warm-heartedness. The wife often talked to me intimately like a friend to a friend. By request of Miss Kingdon she taught me the Lord's Prayer, teaching me a phrase a night. The husband was also friendly, and I can remember him taking me out for a ride on his bicycle, and showing me the road to Taft. They also took a great deal of pleasure in teaching me a few English words.

The end of the school year came; I remember being examined by the Principal herself, and being given a picture instead of an examination report. For the long summer holidays I went to Taft, and during those months there must have been another struggle between Miss Kingdon and my father. I was now about seven years old, and a girls' school could not keep a boy of that age. But the mission had a boys' college with its preparatory school in Isfahan; and it was to that school that Miss Kingdon wanted me to go. But it was one thing for my father to let me go to Yezd, and quite another thing to let me go to another town which to a Yezdi of that day was almost a foreign country. But somehow Miss Kingdon got her way again. This time we hired a donkey, and father and I left Taft in the middle of the night with the small caravan. Many a time I have crossed the distance between Taft and Yezd, but somehow that journey stuck in my mind very distinctly. There is nothing more beautiful in Yezd than its sky at night, and its gorgeous mountains in the early morning and in the evening, with the effect of light and shade on them. I remember that, while sitting on the donkey continuing our journey, I started to recite verses from the 8th Psalm:

> "O LORD, our Lord, how majestic is thy name in all the earth! . . . When I look at thy heavens, the work of thy fingers, the moon and the stars which thou hast established; what is man that thou art mindful of him, and the son of man that thou dost care for him?"

My father, who was always interested in any recitation and poetry, asked me where I had learned all that, and I can never forget the pride with which I answered, "At school in Yezd."

Cars were still fairly new between towns in Persia in those days; but I was lucky enough to sit for 200 miles on a tin full of water in the front of a big lorry where the driver, his assistant, and one or two other passengers were occupying the seat. We arrived in Isfahan at night, and in those days you had to go over one of the famous ancient bridges to enter the town. This was the first time I had seen electric lights, for they had not yet reached Yezd. Rows and rows of lights over the bridge were so fascinating to my eyes that I forgot all the tiredness of the journey. I cannot remember where we spent the night, but I can remember clearly that the next morning I was taken to the little primary school, and its small hostel. There I was handed over to a man who was destined to play a great role in my life. He was the head of the school and his name was Jalil Aqa.

CHAPTER TWO

IN ISFAHAN TO CHRIST: STRUGGLE AND FAITH

"Isfahan Nessf-i-Jahan" is a well known idiom throughout Persia, and it means "Isfahan is half the world"! Isfahan is among the largest towns of the country and no doubt the loveliest. Its history goes back to Cyrus the Great and to the glories of pre-Islamic Iran. There are ruins of ancient fire-temples where the Zoroastrian inhabitants of Isfahan used to hold services in honour of fire and light. The Arab Invasion of Iran in the 7th century made Isfahan into a Muslim town. The most glorious time in its history belongs to the period of the Safavis in the 17th century. Isfahan was made their capital, and they spent their energy, time and talents in making it beautiful. They made a large square in the middle of the town, one of the biggest in the world even to this day, and called it Naqsh-i-Jahan, "the Design of the World". Mosques, palaces and bazaars were built round it. The turquoise-coloured domes of the mosques against the shining blue sky, the old plane trees, and the minarets, form a most romantic picture which once seen will never be forgotten. Today these splendid ancient monuments are surrounded by modern buildings. These have given a peculiar character to the town, a meeting place of East and West. In very few places in Iran have the East and the West met so closely and intermingled so thoroughly as here.

Isfahan has always been a great centre of learning. A lovely theological college from the time of the

Safavis is still in use; here the last king of the dynasty had a royal room assigned to him, for he was particularly interested in religious studies. The people of the town are by nature thrifty and quick-witted, artistic and clever with their hands. Cloth-printing, silver work, miniature painting and tile work have attracted tourists and customers from all over the world. Isfahan is also famous for its lovely and varied kinds of fruit; the river Zayandeh Rud, winding through its plains, makes it possible for the farmers, more fortunate than their brothers in Yezd, to plant trees and sow seeds of many kinds.

Isfahan has a long history of contact with Christianity also. The most recent occasion was when Shah Abbas moved thousands of Armenians from his north-western domains to his capital, Isfahan. On the south bank of the river he built them a small town which the Armenians called Julfa after the original Julfa in their native land. The Armenians have a very independent spirit and are an extremely artistic people. Their contact with the Muslim citizens of Isfahan, however, has been very limited. Even half a century ago, on wet days they were not allowed to cross the bridge which lies between them and the town lest they might make the town unclean. On other days it did not seem to matter, because the medium of uncleanliness was "moisture". Their churches and the crosses over the domes were a certain witness to Christianity to those Muslims who dared to go over to Julfa. But preaching the Gospel openly to Muslims was not allowed, the Armenian Church became more and more inward-looking and enclosed, and lost its evangelistic spirit, if indeed it had any when it was first established in Isfahan.

It was not until the end of the last century, when the Church Missionary Society built a hospital and a school in Julfa, that new contacts began to introduce new life into the ancient community. The missionaries also were not allowed into the town of Isfahan. But soon God opened up the way; a missionary doctor, who was specially endowed with the gifts of gentleness, meekness and friendship, bought a piece of land in the town itself, and started to build a much-needed hospital there. Soon a church was built in the middle of the compound, and this exists to this day.

The little mission school in Julfa was also eventually transferred to the town. The mission bought another large piece of land in another part of the town and built a college there, and called it "the Stuart Memorial College" in memory of a retired bishop from New Zealand, earlier a missionary in India, whose love for the Muslim had brought him to Iran in old age as a missionary.

The mission also started a girls' school next to the hospital compound; but soon they transferred it to a locality nearer to the boys' college, leaving only a small primary school with the colourless name of "The College Branch School". It was to this school that I went when I first arrived in Isfahan. The College Branch School had only four classes, and a small hostel attached to it.

One of the worst things that can happen in missionary institutions is that insincere men and women can deceive themselves and others by pretending that they are Christians, while inwardly and in their homes and among their old acquaintances they are not. The effect of such hypocrisy on the life of a young church is devastating. Although in the church of my childhood sincere, educated and upright Persian Christians were very rare, we students of the College Branch School and its hostel were fortunate to have a man like Jalil

Aqa as our headmaster and teacher. He lacked many things as an educationist and character-builder, but he was not a hypocrite. Through and through he was a sincere man.

By race Jalil was a Cossack. Jalil's father, Khalil, was a colonel in the army of the king of that day, and he was brought to Isfahan to train the local army. Khalil was a Sunni Muslim and had strong tendencies towards mysticism. He took a great deal of trouble over the education of his son Jalil, whose aptitude for learning and artistic abilities soon made him a poet, a first-rate calligraphist and well versed in Persian literature. The wise father saw to it also that his son should learn French and English, which in those days was very rare indeed.

Jalil had something the matter with his chest. The best place to go for treatment was the Christian hospital. There Jalil talked with the Christians and read their Bible. Soon his mystic spirit was attracted by the Person of Jesus Christ, and he gave himself and his abilities to Him and to His Church. The Church in Iran has not since had anyone else quite like Jalil Aqa. He had digested the best of Persian culture, and then had baptized the whole into Christianity. He gave to the Persian Church the best hymns we have, truly Christian and up to the high standard of Persian taste for poetry. He wrote out a number of books and tracts with his own hand: some of these, such as the whole of St. John's Gospel, were photographed and are still in circulation.

Obviously Jalil was the best man to be put in charge of the College Branch School. He soon married a Christian girl, and she ran the little hostel. Like most poets and artists, Jalil Aqa was extremely sensitive and had very little control over his emotions. He had his strong likes and dislikes, and nothing could stop him from saying what he felt about things as well as people.

Jalil's personality and temperament had a great effect on me. Somehow, I soon became a favourite with him, and so a favourite with most of the school and the church. My being a small motherless boy away from home must have appealed to his poetical sensitivity. Also he must have seen in me some likeness to himself, for even at the earliest stages of my education I loved poetry and calligraphy; this always creates love between father and son, teacher and pupil, and friend and friend. The whole programme of the school seemed to consist of calligraphy, Bible teaching and poetry. Other subjects such as arithmetic, music and drawing were either unknown or not important. Our classes were very small and Jalil used to give me a great deal of attention; I soon started to write verses, and to show possibilities of being a good calligraphist. The more I showed signs of progress in these things, the more his exaggerated praises of me increased. He used to compare me favourably with his own sons in our hearing, repeating Jacob's mistake in different surroundings. In other words, he managed to spoil me utterly, and by the time I reached adolescence I was a conceited young fellow. This did not mean that he never punished me. The trouble was that he did not punish me when he ought to have done, and punished me when he ought not to have done. I clearly remember two occasions when I was caned and did not know the reason, except that he was very angry about something.

For summer holidays I used to go home to Taft. For most boys, home and school form part of the same society, and it is natural to pass from one to the other. It was not so for me. It was more of a series of jumps from one side of a ditch to the other. This ditch was the ever-widening gap between my early home and my school life; between those who were responsible for my education and those who cared for me in Taft; and finally the gap between Islam and Christianity. Each year home seemed more different from school and Taft more different from Isfahan. For the first few weeks of the summer holidays, I used to count myself a Christian, arguing with my father and others about my beliefs; but their influence and the whole atmosphere of the village within a few weeks would grow on me and turn me into a Muslim. The Lord's Prayer would turn into the Surahs of Praise and Unity from the Quran; so when I was back again at school after the long summer holidays, I would start as a Muslim and gradually change into a Christian as the influence of the school grew.

This mental and spiritual seesaw went on chiefly during the two summer holidays when I was ten and eleven years old. By the time I was twelve the school influence had outweighed the home influence and I had decided to be a Christian. In Taft I was more aggressively evangelistic than ever! The intensely evangelical atmosphere of our church and school in Isfahan had made me into a conceited little evangelist, who would argue vigorously with his father, brother and the elders of the village.

This was too much for my father and Yahya my brother; and with the pressure of the public opinion of the village they decided not to let me go back to Isfahan. Instead I was sent to a *Maktab*, a sort of one-roomed school usually run by a Mulla. He sits there with his long cane and all the students round him, and somehow he manages to teach them all. But one day was enough for me, and I determined not to go near a *Maktab* again. Whether the Mulla wanted to frighten his new pupil from Isfahan, or whether it was his usual way of chastising I do not know; but I do know that the whole morning was spent in dressing up an unfortunate boy in a most unbecoming way, painting his face red, and taking him round the bazaar of Taft on a donkey. And the whole afternoon was spent in fear and trembling and longing for the evening to come.

As I refused to go to the *Maktab*, my father sent me to the village government school which had recently been started. But God's design for my life was not going to be interfered with. All of a sudden six letters arrived, some addressed to my father and some to myself, all imploring my father to let me go. Two were from Miss Kingdon, who had written both to my father and to my aunts. Another was from Jalil my beloved teacher, who had written in his own lovely handwriting to my father advising him to reconsider his decision. But my father was adamant. "You are still a child," he would argue, "and I am responsible for your religion; at the age of fifteen you will be religiously adult, and then you may rightly decide for yourself . . . I cannot let you go because the village will oppose me." So the answer to all the letters was, No! But Miss Kingdon would not take "No" so easily. She sent to Taft two Christians from the Yezd church, one a lay reader and the other a hospital male nurse, to see my father and persuade him to let me go. My father, overwhelmed by their eloquence, once again took refuge in consulting the Quran. For the second time God showed my father that it would be a very good thing for him to let me go back to Isfahan, and so once again I said goodbye to my relations and went. Saying goodbye to my grandfather, which proved to be for the last time, was particularly touching. He kissed my forehead, his bushy beard covering the whole of my small face, saying, "You won't ever give up your religion, will you?" He meant Islam; but I took it to mean Christianity, and remained faithful to his last piece of advice.

Just then a decree had come from the government ordering the closing down of all foreign primary schools. The College Branch School, which had only four classes, was closed down. But the then Principal of the college had gone to Teheran, to ask permission for the Stuart Memorial College to go on having its fifth class for another year and its sixth for another two years, in order that the students might finish their primary education there. In the end the Principal came back with the permission granted. I think it was in God's plan for me that this permission was given, so that I might finish my primary education in a Christian school. Is not this the right way for a Christian to look at history, seeing the hand of God in all events weaving the pattern of the life of nations and individuals?

I obtained the Government Primary Certificate at the age of thirteen, and then the Stuart Memorial College had to close down its primary school altogether. It was decided that I should carry on with my studies in the secondary part of the college, and go on staying in Jalil Aqa's home. Everything had just been nicely arranged and things were going normally, when suddenly a tragic occurrence disrupted everything. Shokat Khanum, Jalil Aqa's beloved wife, died, and that meant the end of an orderly life for Jalil and his home. His artistic and sensitive nature was so affected by this cruel event that to the end of his life he was never quite himself again.

There is nowhere better for a child than his own

home. There is no one so essential for his growing up into a healthy and whole person as his mother and father. Over and above all this, for healthy growth children need regular food and sleep and loving care. As a boy I was never very strong. I was thin and small, and my somewhat delicate physical condition was not improved by the lack of any responsible person to look after me for a time after Shokat Khanum's death. Everybody was far more interested in my spiritual welfare than in my bodily growth. These they "ought to have done, without neglecting the others" (Lk. 11 : 42).

Shokat Khanum's death took away whatever order and discipline there had been in my life as far as food and sleep and physical comfort were concerned. Most people around me seemed to be much interested in my handwriting, encouraged me to write verses, and were delighted when I learned stories and verses from the Bible. But no one seemed to care what I ate, when I ate, or what time I went to bed! As a result nature gave the danger signal. I started a series of illnesses, sunstroke followed by malaria, and other kinds of fevers. Hospital seemed to become more of a home for me than anywhere else. In my fifteenth and sixteenth years I spent about six months in and out of hospital, and as a result I could not sit for the final examinations of that year.

But there was one person who cared and that was an English missionary, our Sunday School teacher. I owe a great deal to a good many people, but perhaps I do not owe anyone else quite so much as I owe her. When we were still at the little hostel of the Branch School, she used to spend hours with us teaching us new hymns, putting on plays and tableaux for Christmas, and running a Wolf Cub pack as well as organizing a very efficient Sunday School. But my debt to her is not only spiritual and educational; it is material also. Noticing my weakness and seeing me ill so often, she arranged for me to have milk and malt. But although that perhaps saved my life, it did not prove to be enough, for I still went on being ill. As my mother had died of tuberculosis, both this teacher and others gradually came to fear that I might have inherited it; so into the hospital I went for a test. I was then about sixteen years old and was just able to read English a little. The person in charge came and wrote on my chart "No T.B. seen". Out of the hospital I went, but still weak and easily prone to illness.

In the end the missionary pastor of the Isfahan church solved the problem. What I needed more than anything else was to be looked after in a more systematic way. The Stuart Memorial College Hostel was too expensive. To live in a missionary's home they thought was not wise. "Missionaries," they argued with themselves, "do not live a normal life according to the standards of the country," and so if I lived in one of their homes I would be brought up as a stranger in my own country. So I was given a room of my own, quite separate and yards away from any other room in the courtyard. For three years I lived in that room, like Robinson Crusoe on his island. Breakfast and supper I used to have in my room, and lunch I used to eat in the Women's Hospital Nurses' kitchen while chatting with Khadijeh, a charming old woman who was "Jack of all trades and master of none" in the hospital. My missionary friends did really give me a well ordered and disciplined life. For the whole of the first month that I was in their house, the pastor's wife took my temperature morning and evening. For quite a long time the pastor came every night to my room, and very grimly looking at his watch said, "Hassan! Khab!" which means, "Hassan! Sleep!" If my teacher's insistence on my having milk and malt saved my life in childhood, the missionary pastor's insistence on sleep restored health to me in my adolescence.

The mental and psychological damage had, however, been done. Tuberculosis, and the fear of being weak and ill, haunted me for a very long time, and perhaps they will never quite leave me. But for the time being I was a happy lone bird in that room of mine, like a bird in its separate nest in a jungle.

After my second visit to Taft when I was about ten years old, I had decided to follow in my mother's footsteps and become a Christian. Apart from reading the Bible, at the age of eleven or twelve I had finished reading *Pilgrim's Progress* in Persian. Lives of Sadhu Sundar Singh and Kagawa of Japan proved very inspiring, and from those days my one and only desire was to be like them. The teachings of Jesus Christ I came to regard as being higher and lovelier than any I had yet come across. Love, even towards one's enemies, purity in thought and heart, monogamy, the idea of marriage for life, and finally the Christian attitude not only towards life but also towards death made me prefer Christianity to any other religion.

However, our Church would not baptize me as I was not yet eighteen years old. A year before my baptism, at the age of seventeen, I was extremely keen on religion and was fighting bad habits and trying to acquire good ones by resolutions. I still have a book belonging to those days in which there are seventy-seven resolutions recorded; I remember writing them at the end of an inter-church summer school, when I was feeling particularly religious and anxious to be as perfect as possible.

A year later just before my baptism I wrote a letter to my father and brother telling them of my definite desire to follow Jesus Christ in my life. It was a very hard letter both for the writer and the reader. Some of the sentences in it are as follows:

". . . Man cannot please God by fasting, pilgrimage and even prayer. God is not in need of these things, He only wants a pure and strong faith. No one can save himself, but God will save those who seek Him . . . Of course you know that everybody is free to choose his religion for himself, and I will be eighteen soon. I have found the joy and happiness that I want in Jesus Christ . . . Dear father and brother, I know you will be sad and angry when you read this, but this is what I have found out for myself from God, and I hope you also will read from our Mother's Bible which is still in our house. Please, father, do not count yourself responsible for my religion, as I will soon be eighteen and will be legally responsible for myself . . ."

Three months after having written this letter I was baptized. That year and the two following years were the happiest I had yet spent. When I went for my summer holidays that year my father and brother tried their best to convince me that I was wrong. Other people in the village were not very friendly, and I noticed that old friends would pass by without even looking at me. But not so my family. They regarded me as unclean, would not feed with me from the same bowl, would change their clothes and wash ceremonially each time they wanted to say their prayers. Yet they were always loving and hospitable, and this made the cross heavier for me to bear. The only hard thing I heard from my father was when one day he said, "When your letter came telling us of your decision, I dreamt that my right hand was cut off from me, and that means you! You are no longer a part of us!" Yet I prayed for my father and brother and still do so, and they say that they also did and do the same for me.

In Isfahan I was given increasingly more responsibility in the church, with lessons to read in the services, writing and translating new hymns, and so on and so forth. The unconscious happy zeal of those days is unforgettable. In the college I gradually became a senior boy and took an active part in the college Christian Union and the life of our college as a whole. One of the events of those days is worth recording:

I had an argument one day with a boy who was one year senior to me. In the heat of the argument he threatened to beat me up, and I said that as a Christian I would not hit back. He then slapped me very hard on one cheek. I turned my other cheek to him, he slapped again. This was repeated three times. This is what I wrote in my diary that night: "In the afternoon R slapped me on one cheek and I turned the other. He did it again and I turned the other cheek again. At the fourth time he said: 'You must not think because of your religion I am ashamed of what I have done, but I won't slap any more.' As we had two free periods in the afternoon I went into the college chapel and prayed for R. I spoke with God and decided not to tell the Principal; for if I complained to the Principal for revenge, the whole idea of not slapping back would be missed. God revealed all this to me in prayer." But after a few days our Scout Master, a non-Christian, made me go and complain to the Principal, which I did; as a result the College Council was informed and R was asked to apologize to me—a thing which was very difficult for him, for compared with me he had a great deal more of the riches of this world.

There was another year to go before I finished at the

college, and then again came a decree from Teheran demanding the handing over of all foreign educational institutions to the government. Finally permission was granted for a year's respite. It appears very strange that once again the respite was given for me to finish my secondary education in a Christian college!

My last year at the college was a very happy one. I became responsible for a meteorology set that was in the college, and thus earned some money to enable me to go to the hostel which in this the last year of the college had necessarily become very small.

The second world war started in September 1939. I received my diploma in June 1940, when the college and the hostel which had become so dear to me passed out of the hands of the mission and the church.

But God's design for my life continued.

CHAPTER THREE

WITH CHRIST THROUGH DESPAIR: ADVERSITY AND TRUST

Teheran as compared with other ancient towns of Persia is a newly built city. When it was made the capital of the country, over one and a half centuries ago, it was a very small place situated close to the ruins of the ancient and prosperous town of Rey. The father of our present king, Reza Shah, decided to modernize his capital. Within a few years long wide asphalted streets took the place of the old narrow and dusty lanes. Huge and, in many cases, lovely buildings were built in European style with touches of Persian architecture here and there. The Shah, though essentially a soldier, did not forget the necessity of learning. More than half a century before his time the foundation of a University for Teheran had been laid by a wise and keen national leader, but after his death it had all subsided. Reza Shah built a modern university on the north side of the town, and so Teheran University was born, with faculties of medicine, technology, law, literature and so on, mostly on the French system of higher education.

Should I go to Teheran for higher education or not? Where would I live if I went? Would not the atmosphere both in the capital and its university affect my faith in an adverse way? These were some of the questions the Diocesan Council had to deal with in the summer of 1940, for I had put myself at the disposal of the diocese as one who had had a call to the ministry. Finally the Diocesan Council agreed to take a risk. An agreement was drawn up by which the diocese would give me a scholarship annually to enable me to go to Teheran for higher education. In the event of my not wanting to be ordained or work for the diocese later on, I was to pay back the amount I had received from them; this was both fair and wise.

The three years of university life in Teheran were most interesting. For my first year I hired a room in a flat in one of the noisiest streets of Teheran. For my second year I became a paying guest in a friend's home, and for the greater part of my third year I shared a room with an old Isfahan College friend who was also studying in the University, but was living in the Alburz Hostel of the old American Alburz College of Teheran. That year, though my last and so academically the hardest, nevertheless was the happiest. Because of war years the financial situation of the country was not good. Prices started to soar. For three or four years bread was scarce everywhere. Many hours I wasted waiting to buy a piece of bread at the baker's shop, which I could have better spent in a library reading. I tried to start English classes to earn some extra money, but somehow was not successful. Through a friend one of the Teheran daily papers agreed to buy translations for its long columns, and I faithfully went on giving them page after page, but money was not forthcoming. Later on I learned that another man had been adding my wages to his salary, believing that as a fresher in the job I needed to translate without pay for some time!

Secularism was the fashion in the Teheran University of that day. Young people were much more interested in Western Philosophy than in Eastern Religions;

they devoured modern psychology while they were not particularly interested in observing their religious ceremonies. The desire to study economics and books such as *Capital* by Karl Marx and "The Communist Manifesto" was much stronger than that to study the Holy Books of religions.

My simple faith had already been a little shaken during my last year in the Stuart Memorial College through studying elementary practical psychology, but there I was surrounded by wise Christian teachers. One of these had advised me never to give up prayer and church-going, even if the whole thing seemed meaningless at times; I listened to this sound advice. Some may object to this, and say it is hypocrisy to go on praying and going to church while you feel that the whole thing is not real. It is much more honest and brave to leave such things and occupy yourself with the real things in life. But supposing pilots were to leave off controlling their planes whenever they got this strange feeling that the whole thing may be unreal, as the philosophical side in all pilots might lead them to think sometimes! Who would then be safe travelling by air? Surely we do not live only by our feelings! We certainly have to learn to go on with the life of our faith irrespective of how we feel about it.

Besides our own small Anglican church which I used to attend regularly in Teheran, I used to attend the Presbyterian church in the American mission and join in their lively young people's activities. But I strongly believe that, before most young people can appreciate Christian worship and church-going, they need to meet the right *person* who can help them in their faith. One of the older missionaries of the American mission in Teheran was such a person for me at that time. In his quiet, humble and deep way he used to listen patiently to my unending questions, and then would give short simple answers which would keep me thinking for a long time. His wife was always welcoming with a smile, no matter how busy she was. In fact the home of these missionaries in Teheran was a refuge for my confused head and wondering spirit in those days in the disturbed atmosphere of the capital.

The three books of Fosdick, *The Manhood of the Master*, *The Meaning of Prayer*, and *The Meaning of Service*; and later on *Victorious Living* by Stanley Jones, were a great help to me.

Within the intimate circle of my friends in the university I was known as a Christian. Some were interested and some disgusted, but the majority were indifferent and thought that there was something strange about me to be seriously thinking about things religious in the twentieth century!

For summer holidays I used to go to Isfahan and join the Church activities there, especially youth camps and children's special summer schools. I also used to visit my people in Taft, but found the gap between us ever widening.

I graduated in the summer of 1943, and then had to do my military service. As a Christian I was against fighting of any sort. So, before entering the Officers' Training College, as all university graduates had to do I thought it was only honest to let my views be known to the authorities. With the help of a friend I managed to get an appointment with the Chief of the General Staff. He was a kind old man, and this is what passed between us:

"Salam!"

"Salam; what can I do for you?"

"I am a Christian."

"Well, what about it?"

"I am against any kind of fighting."

"There is no fighting going on in our country now."

"But I am a conscript, and must do my military service. I am ready to be trained in any kind of service no matter how dangerous, but it is a waste if I be trained in killing. Because I can never do that."

The Chief of the General Staff then saw for what reason I had gone to him, but said that he could not do anything for me, since it was the responsibility of the Officers' Training College to train me in any line they saw fit. I went out from the General Staff Headquarters straight to the Training College. No one gave me any chance to say anything there, and I suddenly found myself dressed as a cadet to be trained as an infantry officer.

The kind old man in the General Staff had enquired from the friend who had introduced me to him whether I was slightly mad. This is how the world judges the way of Jesus and those who would follow it.

The training in the army was in many ways strange for me. Some of the mottoes we had to learn and make part of our lives I found in exact contradiction to the teachings of Jesus Christ. "See and not be seen! Kill and not be killed!" But the irony of it all was that we were in the middle of the second of two world wars, both of which had been started by the so-called Christian West. Even to-day we are still engaged in advancing the cause of war! May be, if my old friend the Head of the General Staff was alive to-day, he would be prepared to revise his impression of our conversation of that day.

After about four months we were given forms to fill up our particulars. For religion of course I wrote "Christian", and waited for repercussions. One or two days afterwards our commanding officer while on horse-back summoned me to himself in front of the whole company and asked:

"What is your religion?"

"I am a Christian."

"Is your father a Christian?"

"No!"

"Is your mother an Armenian?"

"I have no mother. She died when I was very young. She was not an Armenian, but became a Christian in a mission hospital."

"You should have taken up the religion of your father and not of your mother."

"I have not taken up anybody's religion. I have chosen myself to be a Christian."

"Where and when?"

"During my school days in a mission school in Isfahan."

"Away with you! I cannot trust you any longer."

"As you please, Captain, but if I were you the reverse would have been the case. I could have easily lied and not have written on the form 'Christianity' as my religion, but I did not want to deceive anyone."

He then ordered me to leave him, but I did not notice any signs of unkindness from anyone. What was more, one of our sergeants (they had tremendous powers) drew much nearer to me as the result of this open witness.

During training we had to be on guard for hours, but with very little to guard except long dark corridors. The hymns and the Psalms I had learned by heart in childhood were a great help to me in those hours of uncreative life; it was then that I turned one or two of the Psalms into verse and they are now being sung in our churches.

At last our course of training finished, and I was

commissioned as 2nd Lieutenant staff officer, to be the secretary-interpreter to an American Colonel who had just been appointed adviser to the Isfahan Division. These were my first days "in society" as it were, and it was the first time that I was getting a regular and good salary. It was important at such a time to be near a church and to take an active part in its activities, and which church could be better than one's own church? Isfahan had really become my home, and the members of St. Luke's church there my family. I was very glad to be with them once again, and I used to give the whole of my free time to church activities, finding a great deal of enjoyment in them.

At the end of my military service I offered myself to the diocese as a candidate for the ministry, and was rather surprised when they advised me to go on for some time with my job. My Colonel wanted me very badly, so I made a contract with the government to stay in my job as a civilian secretary-interpreter for another year, with what was then considered to be a huge salary.

But only a few months had passed when the Executive Committee of the diocese asked me to consider employment with a view to being trained for ordination. Not only my Colonel but most of my friends tried to persuade me against breaking my contract. Their argument was that I had a very good chance of collecting a substantial sum of money. "You had better do this first," they would argue, "and then go and join the church or do anything else you like." But I knew that the difficulty would be to know when the sum was "substantial". Also I was vaguely aware of the dangers of money and position, and of how they could unconsciously and gradually choke the spirit within one.

The one difficulty as far as I was concerned was my family in Taft, my father, step-mother and brothers.

They had been very pleased with my recent job, and were hoping that by earning a good salary I would raise the standard of living for the whole family. They hated the idea of my ordination, and indeed it was extremely hard for them. Just imagine the son of a village family in England of the middle ages not only becoming a Muslim, but leaving a good job and deciding to be a Mulla! The turmoil was not only theirs, but mine too and perhaps even more severely. By choosing to follow Christ I had separated myself from them, but now I knew that ordination would mean cutting myself off even more deeply from them, and indeed from almost the entire social life of my own country. The uprooting, loneliness and lifelong inner tension tend to be so terrific that it has led even some Christians to doubt whether it is wise to make converts of individuals, without their families, in non-Christian lands. But Christ said:

> "Do not think that I have come to bring peace on earth; I have not come to bring peace, but a sword. For I have come to set a man against his father, and a daughter against her mother ... He who loves father or mother more than me is not worthy of me; and he who loves son or daughter more than me is not worthy of me" (Matt. 10 : 34–37).

Is it not an amazing thing that such a clear-cut and stern demand should be made by someone in history, and that nearly two thousand years after, it should still carry with it a power to attract people so much that they should respond to it almost literally—as a result making their own all the mental, spiritual and emotional torment which goes with their choice?

It was not easy. But like St. Paul I could not disobey the heavenly vision which I had been seeing throughout my life, no matter what the price might be. Somehow I had always felt like Jeremiah: "Before I formed you in the womb I knew you, and before you were born I consecrated you" (Jer. 1 : 5). And like the psalmist when he said:

> "Truly, thou art my God even from my mother's womb. Truly, marvellous are thy works, and that my soul knoweth right well ... I have said, Thou art my God, My time is in thy hand. Thou hast informed me and taught me in the way wherein I should go. Thou hast guided me with thine eye."

The year the second world war started King George VI of England quoted the following lines in his Christmas broadcast:

> "And I said to the man who stood at the gate of the year: Give me a light that I may tread safely into the unknown! And he replied: Go out into the darkness and put thine hand into the hand of God. That shall be to thee better than light and safer than a known way."

The war ended in 1945, but the future was still unknown. Those lines had a fascination for me, because they conveyed the true meaning of faith in this world. They were my answer to the friends who used to argue that I should prepare myself and my family's future by piling up money in the bank or investing it in land and property. Those lines which had been so helpful to me I translated into Persian verses; they have since become part of the Persian Hymn Book.

My job in the diocese was to work amongst youth, to get on with Christian literature work and to study as much as possible. Outwardly everything seemed all right. I was glad that I had started to fulfil the vocation of my life; and most of the church people were very glad that I had given up a good job to put myself at the service of the church. But inwardly I was not at rest, and I did not know why. I wanted to progress in Christian character, fight bad habits and replace them with nobler ones, but somehow I used to fail horribly. Deep down in my spirit I felt utterly alone and weak. One of the elderly ladies of the mission got very near to me. I used to tell her everything, and used to pour out my difficulties and troubles to her. She acted like a mother and was a great help to me, but the restlessness inside me continued.

After nearly two years it was arranged that I should go to Ridley Hall, Cambridge, for my theological training. This was indeed exciting, and more excitement was added to it when it was suggested by the Near East Christian Council that I should attend the second World Christian Youth Conference at Oslo. I left Teheran in the summer of 1947, and after a fortnight in London I left for Oslo with hundreds of other young people from all over the world.

It was wonderful to see about 1,300 delegates from about 70 countries taking part in a gathering like that. But towards the end of the conference I was shaken to bits when I learned that Christendom was really and truly divided, and that we could not all take part in *one* service of the Lord's Supper. I have not yet got over this shock, and never will; I believe every Christian should feel the same unless and until this tragic division in the Body of Christ is healed.

The first days at Cambridge were intoxicating. The soft green lawns as compared with the long stretches of dry sandy desert of my own country attracted my whole being. The peaceful atmosphere everywhere, the exquisite beauty of the "Backs", the ancient buildings of the colleges with their lovely chapels; and the continuity of the academic life in the place undisturbed for centuries, were sources of wonder, joy and amazement to me. Whenever I climbed my staircase at Ridley, I wanted to bow and kiss the traces of the footsteps of hundreds who had climbed those stairs before me. Somehow the whole thing seemed like a very sweet dream. Here was I, the son of the desert and mountains of Yezd, where life had not changed for the last three thousand years at least, studying theology in Cambridge, the heart of the best that the Western world could offer! I could not get over the wonder and excitement of it all. Somehow I wanted to devour, to breathe in, the whole thing and make it a part of myself.

But when the first excitement passed away I once more came face to face with the realities of life. The old restlessness of the spirit cropped up again and this time in a more intensified way. There was a war inside me, the old war which must have troubled St. Paul when he wrote: "I do not understand my own actions. For I do not do what I want, but I do the very thing I hate" (Rom. 7 : 15). It was as if these words were written for me. How long, O Lord? Where was the power of Christ which strengthened St. Paul to do all things, but did not seem to be strengthening me?

I was becoming lonelier and lonelier within myself. I used to sink down into the lowest state of unbelief and despair, and blamed God for having taken my mother from me so early in my life, for deep down within myself I felt a vacuum for love—to have been loved by someone for what I was, and not for what people would like me to be. The thought of a mother's warm bosom and a father's welcoming arms was so deep an unsatisfied desire within me, that thinking about it used to leave me cold and desolate. I used to blame those who were the cause of my separation from my own people. What right had they, I used to think, to uproot a child from his own environment, his cultural and ethnic background, and let him grow aloof from everything which he could rightly claim to be his own?

Had I stayed in Taft amongst my own people I would probably not have had any of these tensions which were tearing me to pieces. But was it really wrong of Miss Kingdon and others to try to fulfil the wishes of my mother? No doubt in my training mistakes were made, but then in whose training are mistakes not made? I now believe that Miss Kingdon was right and that the missionary movement should be strengthened everywhere. Christ knew better when He said that He had not come to bring peace but a sword. The fact is that, where life is, there must also be suffering. New life involves new suffering. God in His inestimable love and wisdom regarded me as one of those worthy to go through those mental and spiritual torments in order that the new life of Christ might be let loose through me. No one can be the conveyer of this life unless this life has first become part of him, and that cannot happen without suffering. I humbly regard myself as honoured to have gone through all this; only I would say that, "if those days had not been shortened no human being would be saved".

One of my friends had recently committed suicide in London, and that added to my confusion and coloured all my thoughts and emotions. "Why, O Lord, why?" was constantly on my lips. I used to lie awake for long hours letting my imagination be fed by my imaginary misery to such a degree that the thought of suicide started to creep in. The rush of the waves of self-pity and despair was sometimes so tremendous that they used to press streams of tears out of my eyes, and like Job I used to curse the day I was born.

No one seemed to understand me, or if they did I was unable to be helped by them. The religious terms such as "Surrender yourself to Christ", "Pray and He will grant you peace of mind", and "Make your mind blank when you want to go to sleep, and just throw yourself on God" became for me mere clichés void of any real meaning. Had my friends nothing else to offer?

Truly, we are strangely built. How, with all these storms inside me, darkening my spirit and pulling me to pieces, I was able to attend chapel services at Ridley, go to lectures, sit for examinations, and attend meetings and conferences during vacations I do not know. But I do know that I could not have carried on much longer. I was like a ship on a stormy sea whose anchor has been lost, whose compass has been damaged, and whose rudder is not working properly.

But how true are the words of Isaiah for those who have once in their life given themselves up to Him no matter how feebly!:

> "Fear not, for I have redeemed you; I have called you by name, you are mine. When you pass through the waters I will be with you; and through the rivers, they shall not overwhelm you; when you walk through fire you shall not be burned, and the flame shall not consume you. For I am the LORD your God" (Isa. 43 : 1–3).

I wrote a letter to a Christian psychologist asking for help, but no answer came. An undergraduate who was keen on Moral Rearmament knew a Christian leader who had been able to help a number of young people through their difficulties. He advised me to write to him asking for help. I had met him for a few moments at the Oslo conference, and had heard him speak once or twice in London and Cambridge. I took courage and wrote to him. Within a few days the answer came giving me time and place for an interview. In the first interview he let me do most of the talking. He listened to me for about two hours pouring out my heart to him with tears. I felt he loved and understood me, and I was certain that through him I could be healed. During the rest of my stay in England he was in touch with me. Altogether he gave me about six interviews and we often wrote to each other. Here are some quotations from his letters that I have treasured up to this day:

"Now your question why some are called to experience descent into dark depths of despair. First, I think in order that they may be privileged to understand one part of the work of Christ which is hidden from those who have never had such deep experiences. Second, in order that they may be able to help others who through circumstances have to suffer in special ways. God does not waste His material; if He gives a special vocation of suffering He gives a special reward, and special opportunities of service. I think some men have to fight against these temptations to despair all their lives, but if they are sure that God is leading them all the time, they win through: others are completely set free from them . . ."

"Yes, *everyone* in the world needs to be broken-hearted at some time or another—with some it comes before conversion, with others after, but *no Christian* can escape this experience."

"Worrying has become so much a habit with you that it is difficult to stop it easily, but I think you are making progress . . . Never make any promise; simply say to yourself each day, 'Now to-day, if I am faithful to God and trust in Him, He will keep me from evil.' We can't live more than one day at a time, and often your failures are through trying to live further into the future than a man can do . . . There is a great difference between wanting to know and being impatient to know; some things God will never show us, and other things He will show us when His good time has come; in either case we must be patient and let Him do as He wills."

In one of his talks with me my friend suggested that I should read the Psalms, and the Book of Job particularly. The reading of these two books did to my difficulties what sunshine does to snow. All through the book of Job I saw myself speaking:

> "I loathe my life; I will give free utterance to my soul"; "Why dost thou hide thy face, and count me as thy enemy?" "I was at ease, and he broke me asunder; he seized me by the neck and dashed me to pieces"; "Why do the wicked live, reach old age, and grow mighty in power?" "Oh, that I knew where I might find Him"; "But oh, that God would speak, and open his lips to you, and that he would tell you the secrets of wisdom."

And in His great mercy He did. These verses towards the end of the book disarmed me completely:

> "Can you find out the deep things of God? Can you find out the limit of the Almighty? It is higher than heaven—what can you do? Deeper than Sheol—what can you know?" "Who is this that darkens counsel by words without knowledge?" "Where were you when I laid the foundation of the earth? Tell me, if you have understanding"; "Will you even put me in the wrong?" "Will you condemn me that you may be justified?"

And I found myself saying with Job:

> "Therefore I have uttered what I did not understand, things too wonderful for me, which I did not know . . . I had heard of thee by the hearing of the ear, but now my eye sees thee; therefore I despise myself, and repent in dust and ashes."

Repentance was what I needed! Repentance from regarding myself as the centre of the world. The fact was that I had never realized what a self-centred man I really was. All my life I had seen myself through my own created glasses, and never had looked at myself through other people's eyes or in the light of the Cross of Christ. Now, as with Saul of Tarsus, something like scales fell from my eyes and I saw myself as the sort of person I really was: a statue of selfishness, the essence of pride and conceit, and a perfect Pharisee. Serving our small church under the name of "leader", and with the view to becoming a "better future leader", with nobody else quite in the same position as I, completed the work of making me into a Pharisee. And now I had gone to England to become that "better leader" through good training and learning; but a Pharisee cannot learn, he must always teach! How people tolerated me at Ridley I do not know! I shudder to think that there was a time when I truly believed that the whole of our church in Iran depended on me! Apart from my own "wholeness", if I was going to be a useful servant of God for His Church, this awful unconscious pride had to be broken. It is comparatively easy to correct a child who is conceited, but a miracle needs to happen if a conceited young man is to repent. But the God who had a design for my life saw to it that this miracle was performed. By His grace gradually I felt myself coming down from the sanctuary in the Temple of Life where I was constantly thanking God for what I had achieved, to the doorstep of everyday living, asking the Lord to have mercy upon me a miserable sinner.

When this happened everything became different. I then knew what sin really was, what forgiveness meant, and what it cost God to forgive us through the Cross of Jesus Christ. Once I started to *know* these and learn something of the love of God, the healing came gradually. All worry, tension, and restlessness began to vanish away. I found I could even sleep better. People were no more difficult things to live with, but lovable and interesting persons who were objects of the love of God exactly as I was.

Now, how did all this happen? I had read the Psalms and the Book of Job before, and I had heard from others most of the things my Cambridge friend was telling me. Why had I not accepted their word for it? I think what happened was something like this: I had got my faith mainly through missionaries in my own country, and for a time they were enough support for me. In Teheran University I found out that the intelligentsia did not care much for religion. And the people with whom I had most contact in England were mostly missionaries or missionary supporters, and as it is true that even in spiritual and intellectual matters familiarity breeds contempt, I could not be satisfied with them or with what they said. But this friend was different: he was a scholar and a writer; his words and personality gripped me. So when, through the book of Job, I came face to face with the majesty of God and the smallness of man and felt like the psalmist, "What is man that thou art mindful of him?", I was sincerely ashamed of my past presumptuous sins and repented of them. When through the Psalm it dawned upon me that the first step in religion must be a simple trust in God, I could not believe that it was really as simple as all that, and in one of my interviews with my friend I put it to him, "Is it really as simple as that?" And he replied in his confident way, "Yes, it is as simple as that!" I took him at his word; through trusting him I came to learn the meaning of trust in God. I am sure that my faith does not depend on him now, but it did then.

People are brought back to God in diverse ways, and some may not need the help of a person; but in my own experience I believe that it was because I first trusted a person that I was able to trust God. One of my difficulties was that, because of my peculiar upbringing, it had become increasingly difficult for me to trust people. I was living in a world of worry, suspicion, fear and selfishness, which is hell. But God in His mercy saved me from this dreadful state of soul and mind, so that I was enabled to rejoice with the psalmist and sing:

> "I love thee, O LORD, my strength. The LORD is my rock, and my fortress, and my deliverer, my God, my rock, in whom I take refuge" (Ps. 18 : 1–2). "I will rejoice and be glad for thy steadfast love, because thou hast seen my affliction, thou hast taken heed of my adversities ... terror on every side! ... But I trust in thee, O LORD, I say, 'Thou art my God' " (Ps. 31 : 7, 13, 14). "I sought the LORD, and he answered me, and delivered me from all my fears ... This poor man cried, and the LORD heard him, and saved him out of all his troubles" (Ps. 34 : 4–6). "Trust in the LORD, and do good ... Commit your way to the LORD; trust in him, and he will act" (Ps. 37 : 3, 5).

The change in me was so great and deep that I thought I had just been converted, and that before this I had not been a Christian. I told my Cambridge friend this, but he said that I certainly had been converted before; conversion, however, he believed had degrees. His idea was that usually with people, at least in non-Christian lands, their emotions are converted first, then their intellect, and the final stage must be that of the will—the centre of the man's personality. Unfortunately sometimes people stop at the first or second stage and go no further, and that is when the seed is either taken up by the birds of the air, or burnt by the sun, or choked by the thorns. I was sure he was right, and I knew then that my conversion had only reached the second stage and had stopped there. Now the progress of conversion was directed into the sphere of my will.

My vacations I used to spend with my missionary pastor and his wife, who had not gone back to Persia. I used the vacations either for study or visiting friends or going to conferences and meetings, the most important of which was the First Assembly of the World Council of Churches in Amsterdam 1948, to which I went as a youth delegate.

The time to return to my country was gradually drawing near, and I was much looking forward to it. With all the fascination that England, especially Cambridge, had for me, it never crossed my mind not to return to Persia, although at one time I was approached by someone to consider accepting a job in Cambridge itself. The offer was very attractive, but I was sure that I had to return and serve God in my own country.

Before leaving England I went and spent a few days with Miss Kingdon for the last time. We talked about Taft and about my mother, and about the church there. She was delighted and proud to see me, and although she did not agree with my theological outlook it was quite clear that she was very pleased with me. There was something of the look of a proud mother for her son in her face when we said goodbye. That was the nearest to a mother's look, as if to say "I am pleased with you," that I had ever had in my life. Though old and ailing, she came to the station, and in saying farewell for the last time, it was as if she was singing the Nunc Dimittis. She died and went to her Lord, whom she had served so faithfully in this life, soon after I reached home. And so the torch of faith is handed on from generation to generation in most mysterious and unexpected ways.

CHAPTER FOUR

TO ISFAHAN IN MINISTRY: THE CALL TO INTERPRET

On 18 October 1949 (St. Luke's Day), about a month after my return from England, I was made deacon by the Bishop in Iran in St. Luke's Church, Isfahan—the same church in which I had been baptized and confirmed. The bishop was the same friend who had been patiently watching my growth since the time when he was Principal of the Stuart Memorial College. Ten months later I was ordained priest in the beautiful church of St. Simon the Zealot in Shiraz, and soon after that I started my career as pastor of St. Luke's Church, Isfahan.

Marriage seemed to be the last big problem of my life. Our church in Iran being so small in numbers, and the relationship between boys and girls being somewhat limited to meetings between them in official church gatherings, it is not at all easy for young people to find the right partner. My special background and my unusual upbringing added difficulties to the already difficult problem. In Persia marriage is still very much a matter between two families. Whomsoever you marry, you marry the family as well. Was it God's will for me to remain single to the end of my life? If not, how was He going to show a way out? After I had learnt to put my trust, in a more practical way, in God, I surrendered this difficulty also to Him. Then it no longer seemed to be a problem, but an opportunity.

An opportunity to glorify God either by not marrying at all, or by marrying the right person in God's own providence. Here are two extracts from my letters written from England to a friend in Isfahan:

"2 June 1948. The first few months I had difficulty in adjusting myself to the circumstances here. The thought of marriage troubled me. Then I found myself putting Christ second and marriage first. This was definitely wrong. He helped me to put it right. A new thought came to me, namely this—that He may want me never to marry. There is naturally more chance to get to know girls here . . . Getting to know them has helped me very much to realize the difficulties of inter-marriage . . . To me these difficulties are not because of the differences of 'nationality' and 'race', etc. . . . It is because at least one of the partners has to be separated from his or her environment, family and climate, etc."

"8 February 1949. I suppose I am not really in love with anybody—a thing that I should love to be. . . . But I do not worry at all about it, and in spite of this deep desire within me I am quite calm and sane about it; because deep down, perhaps even deeper than the roots of that desire, I am sure that God will lead me in the way He wants me to go. As I have told you before I am quite prepared to remain single to the end of my life, if God wants me to, and no doubt He wants some to do that for Him. That I believe will be my greatest sacrifice to make if He asks for it, but I emphasize again that as far as I know I am ready to make it."

But God who "setteth the solitary in families" did not demand that sacrifice from me. He knew of a girl for me, and in its right time He joined us together in Holy Matrimony. She was Margaret, the youngest daughter of my bishop, who like her mother had been born and spent most of her time in Persia. We were married in June 1952 in the heat of anti-British propaganda during the oil crisis, and thus through the waves of hate and slander we showed that:

> "In Christ there is no East or West,
> In Him no South or North,
> But one great fellowship of love
> Throughout the whole wide earth."

I, who had always felt lonely, and had been unconsciously struggling to belong somewhere, unbelievably found myself part of a family in a way of which I had not dreamed before. After six years of happy married life and with three children, I can now witness that He who had guided me all through life in strange ways guided me rightly and wonderfully in this important step as well. Some friends who know me intimately tell me that, second to my conversion, my marriage has been the biggest miracle in my life, and I think I agree with them. Truly, as the psalmist says: "Thou hast multiplied, O LORD my God, thy wondrous deeds and thy thoughts toward us" (Ps. 40 : 5).

But is this the end of my story? In some ways, Yes; my somewhat sad childhood is a thing of the past, the ups and downs and the emotional restlessness of my adolescence have passed away, my mental and spiritual struggles seem to have settled down, and I seem to be doing what God in His providence all this time has been preparing me for, i.e. to serve His Church in my own country in the best way I can. But in some other ways it is just the beginning.

I feel, like Abraham, that, "The LORD, the God

of heaven, who took me from my father's house and from the land of my birth, and who spoke to me" (Gen. 24 : 7), wants me to proclaim His mighty works of salvation to my own people.

Here I feel I ought to say something for those who doubt the value of preaching the Gospel of the Love of God to the Muslims. It is the right of every man to hear what we believe to be the truth, more especially if that truth is the amazing story of the Cross. It is our duty to tell that story as best we can. The response is not really our concern. How hard it may be for those who accept it is also not our concern. Our poets have sung a great deal about the adventure of love—how a true lover should be prepared to sacrifice everything and endanger all he has for the beloved. Surely the love of God should not kindle a lesser fire in the heart of man than that. If you take away the risks and dangers in the way of love, very little will remain. If you take away the Cross from Christianity, nothing worth while remains. Why should the Muslims be deprived of the privilege of carrying the Cross if they want to? And they cannot possibly want that, unless they are really put in touch with it.

But what is the best way to do that? Fortunately a great deal of scholarly work has been done on the interpretation of Christ to Muslims, and to this I do not wish to add. But for the rest of this chapter I want to state briefly and humbly my own religious convictions and explain how I arrived at them, and how I try to explain them to my Muslim friends.

With regard to my religious beliefs, I cannot say precisely when one belief was shattered by another, and how long I had to wrestle with any particular idea before accepting it. To put it briefly, I have had to travel in my mind from Islam to Christianity and from both to agnosticism, and then back again to the foot of the Cross of Jesus Christ.

Religious liberty is a popular subject these days. Different countries and different regimes and religious systems interpret it differently. Apart from the famous verse in the Quran, "There is no compulsion in religion" (Surah 2 : 256), the way traditional Islam has interpreted religious liberty has been to give freedom to the followers of other main religions in Muslim countries to remain what they are, or to change their religion, if they so wish. But Muslims have had to remain Muslims. This has been, and I presume still is so, in the Arab countries where Islam is the very essence of racial and national life. In Persia, where Islam was introduced by the Arab invaders, the story has been somewhat different. The Persian mind has often rebelled against this limitation of movement. Shi'ite religion, which is the type of the Muslim religion prevalent in Persia, is in itself a rebellion against the orthodox Arab Islam. Our poets such as Omar Khayyam and others have broken this cage of the denial of liberty to become something else, and have soared into the limitless space of free thinking. In modern times this has become even easier than before. Our present day literature is being flooded with all kinds of ideas and thoughts foreign to Islam. A fellow-student in the University of Teheran was so much taken up with abstract philosophy that he found he could not believe in God and remain honest to his way of thinking. After he came out of the University and wanted to be employed, he even went so far as to write on his employment form "Agnostic" for his religion. He was questioned, but when the authorities saw that he was honest about it, they gave him the job. However, this is a very rare and unusual case.

Persia has signed the Charter of Human Rights of the United Nations, and thus has potentially agreed to freedom of religions, as the modern world understands it to-day. We have, therefore, sufficient freedom of thought in Persia to-day to follow religious truth wherever we see it, and to interpret it to others in the way that it has come to us. Therefore let us start our task of interpretation from the origin of all things.

GOD. As a very small boy I remember one evening my elder brother and I were on the roof of our house in Taft talking about God. There was a big basket turned upside down and put over some milk and cheese to keep them cool during the night. My brother was telling me of the attributes of God. He suddenly turned to me and said, "God is light, all light, a big light, as big as that basket—only all light!" Later on I learned more philosophical terms about God from my father and others—that He is Great, He is One, He is Eternal, He does not beget and He is not begotten, and so on and so forth. I learnt that He has some positive attributes such as Wisdom, Power, Life, etc.; and some negative attributes also, e.g. He is not Compound, He is not Matter, He cannot be seen, He has no Partner, etc. Later on, in Christian schools the idea of the Fatherhood of God and of His Love was added to my conception of God.

But when the waves of doubt came, they swept all the above suggestions aside. Such questions as these used to press on my mind: Was there really a God? Why did He create this world with all its defects and imperfections, cruelties and injustices? Why should floods, earthquakes and famines kill off thousands and millions of people, men, women and children? Where was God's greatness then? Why should people suffer physical pain for years and then die without having enjoyed their life at all? Why should people be tormented because of sins committed by others? Where was God's Love? What was the purpose of the whole thing? As one of our poets has said:

> Where we must go, we do not know;
> Nor why we came; nor why we go.
> Though many sought with stress and strain,
> Yet none could make this riddle plain.

Even if there was a God, how were we to know Him? Did He really care for His world? Was there a general and coherent scheme of things, or was there really no purpose in life?

The fact that I was told that God was one, unchanging, merciful and that He was not compound and not matter and not visible, did not make the slightest difference to my essential problems. How can these terms heal the man who is sick at heart? I was tired of words and terminologies and wanted a healing touch, an act of love, a contact.

I could not very well trust a God who only reveals Himself through nature, through the prophets, and through books and systems of law. How about nature's cruelties? How about the sin and selfishness of the prophets? For although the general belief in Islam is that the prophets are sinless, their lives and their writings do not confirm that. It became obvious to me that if there was a God, He should take the initiative, and reveal Himself personally to man.

It was the fact of the Incarnation which made me fall in love with Christianity. "God was in Christ reconciling the world to himself" (2 Cor. 5 : 19). To a Muslim the very idea of God becoming man is blasphemous, but it was this "blasphemy" that saved me from unbelief. To me it came to be the most natural thing. Stories are told of Shah Abbas and how, in order to get to know his poorer subjects, he used to dress up as a poor man—as a dervish—and thus go among them. This gracious act he was able to do precisely because he was king and by such an action nothing was taken away from the glory of his kingship. If we admire such action in human beings, why should we not admire it in God? A God whom we can explain fully and satisfactorily may satisfy our minds, just as a poet's work, for example, gives satisfaction to him. But then that will not be the God who has created us; this is the product of our own minds; we have created Him—a mental idol.

"In the beginning was the Word. . . . And the Word became flesh and dwelt among us." (Jn. 1 : 1, 14.) We cannot understand how, but as with so many things in life we can appreciate why. I cannot see any blasphemy in this gracious act of God. Not to believe in the Incarnation gets rid of a mystery, but it will not solve any problems. Believing in the Incarnation is believing in a mystery, but a mystery which solves many problems: the world and the whole creation belongs to God and He loves it. Sin and evil have entered in and are playing havoc. If love is a true and able love, it must be able to pour out itself to save the beloved; Christians say that was why "God so loved the world that he gave his only Son, that whoever believes in him should not perish but have eternal life" (Jn. 3 : 16).

How can we sinful mortals have contact with God Almighty? The Christian answers: "No one has ever seen God; the only Son, who is in the bosom of the Father, he has made him known" (Jn. 1 : 18). Through the birth of Jesus Christ, God broke into human history and revealed His true character. He was not only great and mighty, He was meek and lowly:

> "Have this mind among yourselves, which you have in Christ Jesus, who, though he was in the form of God, did not count equality with God a thing to be grasped, but emptied himself, taking the form of a servant, being born in the likeness of men" (Phil. 2 : 5–7).

Only the God who would enter His creation in the form of a servant in order to heal our ills is irresistible. He is for me.

One of the greatest problems of Christianity for the Muslim mind has been, and still is, the Trinity. When I was finding it difficult to believe in God at all, it did not make any difference whether He was a mathematical unity or a personal Trinity. But when my faith in God was established, I found I could get nearer to a God who was a complex person than to an abstract philosophical idea and a mathematical unity. It became quite obvious to me that by the Trinity, "Father, Son and Holy Spirit", Christians meant one God in three persons and not three separate deities— "God, Jesus and the Virgin Mary", as some Muslims tend to think. It never even occurred to me that the words Father and Son had any physical meaning, or that "begotten not created" had a literal and material interpretation. I had often heard the titles of "The Hand of God" and "The Lion of God" used for Ali, the prophet's son-in-law; and another title of the same kind for Imam Hussain, Ali's son, and knew that they had spiritual meanings, even when I was a very small child.

One of the famous poets of Isfahan, Hatef by name, tried his best to understand the Holy Trinity. In a long and lovely poem about the unity of God, he refers to a visit to a Christian church and a discussion there with a Christian friend about the Trinity, and at the end of that part, in exceptionally beautiful language, he says:

> While in these matters occupied were we,
> The church bells seemed to peal this solemn chant—
> God is but One: there can no other be;
> One is the Lord; and there is none but He!

Hatef's poem does not fully explain the Christian doctrine of the Trinity, but it lifts it high above the common understanding by Muslims of this doctrine. It was a great help to me, and I am sure it can be to many others.

God in Islam has many names, and each of those "Beautiful Names", as they are called, tries to convey a different aspect of the Almighty. It is more or less the same in Christianity: God the Father, God the Son and God the Holy Spirit are three different names for the One God; and each of these names reveals a different aspect of the complex personality and the mysterious oneness of God. A piece of wood is one piece of wood, it can be broken into any number of pieces of wood, each of them still being a piece of wood. That is one kind of unity. But in the higher scale of life unity gets more complex. If you cut an ant into two pieces, you no longer have your one ant. One of our leading Christian men is a Persian-Christian-Jew, but he is only one person, and each of those names signifies a different aspect of his personality. Surely if we are so complex and yet are one, our Creator cannot be less than that? Even if we cannot understand God fully, once we know Him in this way we cannot be satisfied with any other way.

Some people tend to think that Muslims have one God and Christians another. While I agree that the two concepts are very different indeed from each other, I cannot agree that they really worship two utterly different gods. At least, the way it happened with me was that my faith in a Christian God was related to my early childhood's faith in a Muslim God. When through the Book of Psalms and the Book of Job I learnt anew the meaning of trust in God, and came to worship Him at the foot of the Cross, the basis of it all was the same God my brother was trying to teach me about with the help of the simile of the big basket of light, and my father through the Muslim philosophical terms. I never had a sort of complete "brain-wash", as it were, of my past faith in God; neither did I think it was necessary to do so. It was when I really put my trust in God that I started to study and experience the different conceptions of Him in the two religions. I knew that a God whom I could define with human knowledge, reason and logic would not be enough. Nevertheless my spiritual pilgrimage in the faith in the Christian God was not absolutely disconnected with what was already in me. Christianity took me beyond human reason and logic into the realm of God's glory and God's own ways. I learnt not to judge God on human principles, but rather to trust Him just as an infant trusts its mother. Once I had put my trust in such a God, life was no more made up of disconnected incidents and beliefs without one pattern. All the bits and pieces of the jigsaw puzzle of life fell into their right places, once I had found the key pattern of personal relationship with a personal God through Jesus Christ.

SIN, REPENTANCE AND FORGIVENESS. For a Muslim everything he does counts with God; if it is a good act it goes to his credit, and if it is a bad act it goes to his debit. The balance will decide where he will go after life, to heaven or to hell. Good things are doing such things as saying your prayers regularly, fasting diligently, helping the poor generously and so on and so forth. You are expected to obey all the religious laws and such obedience counts to your credit. Bad things are those things which are against the law. It seems as though in Islam human nature by itself is neutral, neither bad nor good. If you add more individual good acts you are good, but if your individual bad acts, "sins", increase, you have become bad and sinful. I did not find this conception of human nature conform to my experience. It was not the individual acts from outside which made me bad or good; the trouble was that I found myself so bad that I could not do anything which could be called good at all. Even my best intentions were coloured by selfishness. Here I found the Christian idea of sin and its insight into human nature much more true to my experience. Sin in Christianity is not particular actions, it is that condition in man which produces those actions. It is not breaking the law of God, it is putting yourself in place of God. Sin in Christianity is not like dust on your clothes that you can shake off whenever you want; it is something dirty which has soaked in so deep that you cannot even wash it off. Nothing from outside makes us sinful, it is because we *are* sinful that we cannot help but commit sin. That is why man by himself cannot save himself. I felt I could never fulfil all the religious laws of Islam. But, even if I was able to, the result would have been a kind of man further away from God than ever before. For in such a situation I would have been the creditor and God the debtor, and such a relationship between man and God is unthinkable. God still loves such a person, but the man's pride prevents the rays of God's love from reaching him.

How can we be saved from such a dreadful situation?

Obviously we have to repent. What is repentance? Our conception of repentance is necessarily closely connected with our idea of sin, because it is our sins that we have to repent of. In Islam this means being sorry for the things we ought to have done and have not done, and for the things we have done and ought not to have done. Repentance in Christianity means an absolute change of direction. It is getting up and opening the door to the One who is standing and knocking outside. It is dying to oneself, and being born again—a new creation!

One of the names of God in Islam is: "The Merciful Forgiver". But the system of forgiveness is not quite clear. It seems as though God forgives those whom He will, and does not forgive those whom He will not. The prophet and the saints may intercede for you. Good works are the best guarantee, but nothing is quite certain.

In Christianity forgiveness has nothing to do with our goodness and with our good works. It is a free gift from the God of Love to sinful man, and it has one condition only, and that is to trust the God who gives it:

> "For there is no distinction; since all have sinned and fall short of the glory of God, they are justified by his grace as a gift, through the redemption which is in Christ Jesus" (Rom. 3 : 22–25). " . . . even we have believed in Christ Jesus, in order to be justified by faith in Christ, and not by works of the law, because by works of the law shall no one be justified" (Gal. 2 : 16).

THE PROBLEM OF SUFFERING AND THE CROSS OF JESUS CHRIST. Everything in Christianity revolves around the Cross. It is the key by which we can unlock the mysteries of God, Incarnation, Sin and Forgiveness, Suffering and Salvation; and yet it is itself the greatest mystery of all. It is more than a mystery, it is "a stumbling-block to Jews and folly to Gentiles, but to those who are called ... the power of God and the wisdom of God" (1 Cor. 1 : 23–24).

The biggest difficulty in the way of my religious life and belief in God was the problem of suffering. It was belief in the Incarnation which roused my love towards God. It seemed to me to be the most natural thing for God to do—Himself to come down and share our sufferings. He could not be less than a good shepherd. But a good shepherd, Christ tells us, lays down his life for the sheep; He said that He was Himself the Good Shepherd, and at Golgotha He proved this to be true.

It is very hard for the Muslim to believe that God would allow a Prophet of His (for they so regard Jesus) to be ridiculed and killed by sinful men. He thinks that God must show His victory over His enemies as we understand the meaning of victory. That is why Islam believes that God did save Christ, by putting somebody else in His place on the Cross, and rescuing Him from that shameful death. But, once one believes in the Incarnation as the only way of Gods' expression of love in the fullest way, one rather expects such an event as the Cross to be the outcome. If Love meets sin and rebellion, the result cannot be anything but suffering. And it is only through the suffering of love that true healing comes. Thus the problem of suffering and pain for me was raised into the higher levels of the spiritual world. It was no more a thing to grumble about constantly. It became a thing to accept and bear humbly, and thus to let out some spiritual energy into the world.

A piece of work may be an extremely hard and unpleasant thing, but we cease to grumble once we see our king side by side with us trying to shoulder the job. This was how the problem of suffering was solved for me. Suffering can be used as one of the means through which the glory of God can shine—just as particles of dust lend themselves to the pure light of the sun, when it shines in columns through the holes of the covered Persian bazaars.

At the foot of the Cross I found healing, and a new energy and purpose for life. I felt somewhat as one of the characters of Margaret Irwin felt when she was asked: "Why did you take vows?" "Because," she answers, "the story of the God who gave up His Godhead and His human life for the world of humans has always moved me, not with sorrow or pity but with exaltation. Could anything be more glorious than to have so much to give, and give it all?" (*The Bride*, Margaret Irwin).

I can never understand *how* God Almighty came into the world and allowed the Cross to happen to Him, but somehow deep down I can, a little bit, understand *why* He did that. I can never understand how the sin of man is forgiven on the Cross; but when I look at Him on the Cross and try to understand His love, His intentions, and His way of fulfilling His purpose, I cannot but fall down and cry bitterly: "O Lord, have mercy upon me, a miserable sinner", and hear His forgiving voice saying: "Come to me, all who labour and are heavy-laden, and I will give you rest" (Matt. 11 : 28).

Unfortunately the actual way of the Cross has been hidden from the Muslims. Christians have accused the Muslims of resorting to the sword for the spread of Islam, but they themselves have used it to their own purposes. How can a Muslim understand the Cross when he can still remember the Crusades, not to mention the last two world wars? No; we have to admit that we have failed Him and His ways; but that is where the hope arises: We *can* admit that we have failed Him and His ways. When Christians have taken up the sword it has been against their Lord and His ways, and they ought to repent. But taking up the sword in defence of Islam has been and still is a duty.

Ordinarily in the world there are three ways of winning people to your side: (1) Give them what they desire; bread, comfort, pleasure, etc. (2) Make it impossible for them to be able to say "No" to you, bewitch them, hypnotize them with clever lies and irresistible propaganda. (3) Force it on them by any means you can. Jesus was tempted to use one or all of the above three ways, and He rejected them all. "Begone, Satan!" He said to the tempter in the wilderness, and it is written that "the devil left him" (Matt. 4 : 10–11).

Since He had rejected the ways of the world and of the devil, the only course open to Him was to found a new way, the way of perfect love, which is necessarily the way of the Cross. Love must be given and accepted freely. When His disciples wanted to force their way into a village that would not let them in, He said to them, "You do not know what manner of spirit you are of; for the Son of man came not to destroy men's lives but to save them. And they went on to another village" (Lk. 9 : 55–56, R.S.V. note).

He would not resort to force and show off His powers, as people expected Him to do, and that is why "He was despised and rejected by men: upon him was the chastisement that made us whole, and with his stripes we are healed" (Isa. 53 : 3, 5). As the Arabic idiom puts it: "Kings are known of their conquests." The way Christ stood up to hatred, meanness, loneliness, and the agony of the Cross without yielding even for one moment, and finally shouted the victory cry: "It is finished" (Jn. 19 : 30), and the way this victory was openly proclaimed to the world in His resurrection, reveals the quality of the victory of the King of Love over sin. But this victory also reveals the depth of man's sinful nature—not only of those who took part in the original crucifixion, but of me also. I see that the same kinds of sins are part of me: the apostles' weakness and fear, the traitorous heart of Judas, Caiaphas' cunning ways of executing his own policies, Pilate's love of position. The Cross is like a spiritual X-ray apparatus by which we can see our inward parts, and be truly ashamed, and become really humble.

The Christian message that God is somehow in the midst of the sufferings of His world is the only satisfactory answer for me to this mysterious problem. Christians believe that the whole creation is somehow defective, and that God Himself is in it doing reconstruction work; we can be His co-workers if we want to, provided that we share in the toils involved:

> "It is the Spirit himself bearing witness with our spirit that we are children of God ... *provided we suffer* with him in order that we may also be glorified with him ... We know that the whole creation has been groaning in travail together until now; and not only the creation, but we ourselves, who have the first fruits of the Spirit, groan inwardly as we wait for adoption as sons" (Rom. 8 : 16, 17, 22, 23).

BASIS OF CONDUCT. One question our Muslim friends often ask us is: "If you are saved by grace, and your works do not effect your salvation, and if you have no set laws to govern your life, what is then the basis of conduct in your religion?" For a Muslim everything is laid down, from the smallest detail of the individual life to the big social, economic and political questions. Humbly we have to say that, while Christianity attaches tremendous importance to the welfare of the people and to society as such, first and foremost Christianity aims at the individual. Each individual must be born again. The more there are of such new-born individuals in a society the nearer to God that society will be. Those form the Church, and the Church of Christ in any society is the salt of that society and should play the role of the salt, to be antiseptic.

Nations have their parliaments and national assemblies. These organizations lay down necessary rules and regulations according to the needs of the time. The way Christians can influence society is by entering into its life and affecting it. The more Christians get into the parliaments of their countries, the more Christian the laws of their countries will become. For example, in no country of the world are the laws of marriage set exactly according to the mind of Christ, for the simple reason that only real Christians want to obey the mind of Christ in this question, and to accept the principle of life partnership of two individuals—a union in God of two human beings. But the laws of those countries which have an effective Christian minority within them are nearer to the mind of Christ than those which have not such a minority.

But what then governs the life of the individual? A Muslim's duty is set for him almost in everything. He knows how many times in a day he should say his prayers, he knows exactly what words to use for his prayers. He knows what things are clean for him and what things are not. For example, wine to Muslims is an unclean thing, and they are most surprised to find that, according to the Gospels, the first miracle of our Lord is the turning of water into wine.

Christians have no table of "clean" and "unclean" things. We are not under a law, we are under grace, "for the written code kills, but the Spirit gives life" (2 Cor. 3 : 6). It is the child and the servant who need codes of conduct and rules and regulations about everything, but our Lord has called us "friends" (Jn. 15 : 15). Nevertheless, Christ has laid down the principles of conduct and life for us. The two greatest principles are, "Love the Lord your God . . . And love your neighbour" (Matt. 22 : 37, 39). The other principles can be found elsewhere in the New Testament, especially in St. Matthew's Gospel, chapters 5, 6 and 7.

But the norm and the standard of all conduct for us is Jesus Christ Himself. We are to imitate Him in everything. This does not mean that we have to copy Him in superficial things. It means trying to discover His mind and His ways in every situation. We cannot do that by ourselves; the Holy Spirit which is His promise and is ever-present with us helps us in this:

> "And I will pray the Father, and he will give you another Counsellor, to be with you for ever . . . He will teach you all things, and bring to your remembrance all that I have said to you" (Jn. 14 : 16, 26).

In Islam you have to try to be a good religious man by your own efforts, by saying your prayers, reciting the Holy Book, by remembering God on every occasion, and by many other things. In Christianity it is the Holy Spirit of God who does it all. Goodness in Christianity is the fruit of the Spirit within us, and ought to come out unconsciously through our keeping contact with Him (Gal. 5 : 22).

The whole purpose in life for the Christian is: "This is the will of God, your sanctification" (1 Thess. 4 : 3). We cannot make ourselves holy, only He who dwells in us and we in Him can make us so. "Abide in me, and I in you. As the branch cannot bear fruit by itself, unless it abides in the vine, neither can you, unless you abide in me" (Jn. 15 : 4).

The word "Islam" has the most beautiful religious meaning—absolute surrender to God. Christianity demands the same sort of surrender to God. What is the difference, then? Christians regard it their duty to *discover* the will of God afresh in every situation, and fulfil it with the help of the Holy Spirit, no matter what the cost may be. For the Muslim the amount of the will of God necessary for his life *has been revealed* once for all through the Quran. New commentaries can be made on the Word of God, but not new discoveries of His Will. What you cannot discover through the Quran and Law, you cannot discover at all; you have to surrender to what is already revealed, that is the "Qismat", the destiny for you and the world.

Our model in life is Jesus Christ Himself. Jesus reveals whatever is necessary for us to know of God. In Islam the Prophet makes no extraordinary claim. He is the last prophet in the series of many, but he regards himself as an ordinary man. For Christians Christ is God who "has visited and redeemed his people" (Lk. 1 : 68). The prophets like John the Baptist were only "the voice" (Jn. 1 : 23); but the word of Christ is "I AM" (Jn. 8 : 58), which is the name for God. He said, "He who believes in me, though he die, yet shall he live, and whoever lives and believes in me shall never die" (Jn. 11 : 25–26).

Our love must be like His love, "Love one another as I have loved you" (Jn. 15 : 12). This kind of love is freely given to all—not only to our fellow-believers (e.g. Lk. 10 : 25–37). To Him everything in His Father's world was clean; the responsibility of using things is upon us, not upon things. The wine in itself is neither bad nor good; things in themselves are not moral, and badness and goodness are essentially moral values. Cleanliness and uncleanliness have to do with our hearts (Mk. 7 : 1–23). We must serve as He served, and to the same limit that makes us walk side by side with Him to Golgotha where they nailed His hands to the Cross, and yet we hear Him saying: "Father, forgive them; for they know not what they do" (Lk. 23 : 34). I have found no such example of sacrificial service and pure love anywhere else.

THE SCRIPTURES. Muslims believe that the Jews and the Christians are "the people of the Book". They know of the "Towrat" for the Jews and the "Injil" for the Christians. But when they see our Bible they get puzzled. They see a small library under one cover—books written by different people at different times. And as for the Gospels, they are most puzzled: why should there be four different Gospels? And why should the letters of an apostle to churches be included in the Holy Book of the Christians? To them the Quran is the eternal speech of God. It existed before the prophet Muhammad and it was only revealed through him. Even if the Bible was what Muslims expected a Holy Book to be, it would still be out of date to-day, like a bank-note belonging to an old dynasty which is now out of currency. But now they believe that the Bible is not only out of currency, but also that it has been tampered with; and somehow the present "Injil" is not the true "Injil".

The only way to show that it is not out of date is to show them its currency, not only by opening Bible

Society depots, but by "hearing, reading, marking, learning and inwardly digesting it". Then we can explain the different conception we have of the nature of a Holy Book. To use it is inspiration, not automation; it is co-operation between God and man. The Bible is the record of God revealing Himself to man, and of man responding to that revelation. It is, as it were, the minutes of the meetings of God with mankind written by different secretaries. Each secretary's impression will be different from that of the others, but this does not mean that they are not a true description of those meetings.

As for the Gospels, we have to explain that the word "Injil" does not mean a book, it means Good News; and the real "Injil" is Jesus Christ Himself. The four Gospels are an attempt by four chosen artists to give their impressions of the one "Injil". It is the Gospel *according* to . . ., not the Gospel *of* . . . We have to stress the fact that Jesus Christ did not bring a book with Him from heaven, nor did He write any when He was on earth—there was no need for that. When lovers are together, is there any need for writing letters? The four Gospels were written by four chosen men to give the result of the encounter of a "God-Man" with men; and the Epistles are the explanations of what happens and what ought to happen when groups of men put themselves at the disposal of this divine-human personality.

There are many terms and expressions that we cannot understand when we first read the Bible, but any worth-while book is like that. This should not hinder us from diligently studying it, with the help of others, and many other books which have been written about it.

Finally we have to impress on Muslims the fact that there is no historical evidence whatsoever of Christians having changed their "Injil". Is such an act at all possible? Would not at least one copy of the original remain somewhere? The new discoveries of ancient manuscripts and the careful scientific research on the subject have made it impossible to take seriously the idea that the Gospels have been changed.

The Bible is still the best seller, and a book which has been translated into more languages in this world than any other book; it has given and is giving light and life to millions of people from all nations, races and types.

> "Let this be recorded for a generation to come, so that a people yet unborn may praise the LORD" (Ps. 102 : 18).

But words alone cannot bring the Muslim to the foot of the Cross. No amount of interpretation in the abstract brings the Muslim to feel with those in the boat who "worshipped him, saying, 'Truly you are the Son of God'" (Matt. 14 : 33). Christians must show in their lives how Christianity is in truth the incarnation of the love of God. Most of the Muslims I know who have followed Christ have done so because of the sacrificial life and sustained love of some Christian friend. You cannot bring the Muslim to Christ unless you love him personally.

The heart of Christianity is the Cross of Jesus Christ; but this Cross is often hidden in clouds of hatred, suspicion, hardness of heart and pride, which prevail in the world among the sons of men. To dispel these clouds, and disclose the real Cross, calls for more than preaching and teaching. It demands the bearing of the Cross in daily life. This is to go on loving when love seems impossible, and working when no result yet appears.

But there is more. No individual, however saintly,

shows the love of God in Christ fully. Its interpretation needs the community of the faithful—the people of God. The Church where two or three are gathered together in His name—this is the core of the matter. What a tremendous role is theirs, not least when their gathering together is in the midst of a world where for centuries Islam has prevailed!